T0129745

JESUS
Is for Real,
and There Is
POWER
in His Name

JERRY GASPARD

WESTBOW
PRESS®
A DIVISION OF THOMAS NELSON
& ZONDERVAN

Copyright © 2018 Jerry Gaspard.

All rights reserved. No part of this book may be used or reproduced
by any means, graphic, electronic, or mechanical, including
photocopying, recording, taping or by any information storage retrieval
system without the written permission of the author except in the
case of brief quotations embodied in critical articles and reviews.

WestBow Press books may be ordered through
booksellers or by contacting:

WestBow Press
A Division of Thomas Nelson & Zondervan
1663 Liberty Drive
Bloomington, IN 47403
www.westbowpress.com
844-714-3454

Because of the dynamic nature of the Internet, any web addresses or
links contained in this book may have changed since publication and
may no longer be valid. The views expressed in this work are solely those
of the author and do not necessarily reflect the views of the publisher,
and the publisher hereby disclaims any responsibility for them.

Any people depicted in stock imagery provided by Getty Images are
models, and such images are being used for illustrative purposes only.
Certain stock imagery © Getty Images.

ISBN: 978-1-9736-4307-4 (sc)
ISBN: 978-1-9736-4306-7 (e)

Library of Congress Control Number: 2018912360

Print information available on the last page.

WestBow Press rev. date: 05/20/2024

Scripture quotations marked (NLT) are taken from the Holy Bible, New Living Translation, copyright ©1996, 2004, 2015 by Tyndale House Foundation. Used by permission of Tyndale House Publishers, Inc., Carol Stream, Illinois 60188. All rights reserved.

Scripture quotations marked (NIV) are taken from the Holy Bible, New International Version®, NIV®. Copyright © 1973, 1978, 1984, 2011 by Biblica, Inc.™ Used by permission of Zondervan. All rights reserved worldwide. www.zondervan.com The "NIV" and "New International Version" are trademarks registered in the United States Patent and Trademark Office by Biblica, Inc.

Scripture taken from the New King James Version®. Copyright © 1982 by Thomas Nelson. Used by permission. All rights reserved.

Scripture taken from the King James Version of the Bible.

Prince of Peace
Portrait by Akiane Kramarik

Akiane's parents were loving, idealistic, poor, and atheist. At age four, Akiane had a vision of God, Jesus, angels, and heaven. At age eight—equipped with her visions, paintbrushes, and a ladder—she completed a four-foot-tall oil painting of Jesus, which she titled *Prince of Peace*. This is considered Akiane's first masterpiece. Besides painting, Akaine loves to write poetry, play the piano, sew, fashion design, and travel.

You can view and purchase Akaine's art work at Art-Soulworks.com or call (888) 308-8659.

Contents

Introduction

My name is Jerry Gaspard, and I reside in Forked Island, Louisiana. I have been a Christian for many years. I love to spend time reading my Bible, worshipping the Lord, and praying. I treasure the time I spend with the Lord. He gives me revelation, wisdom, peace, and joy.

Most of my life was far from peaceful and joyous. I struggled with depression and have also suffered from addiction to pain medication and major bipolar episodes. I spent three years of my life out of my right mind, but during that turmoil, God was faithful when my faith had run out. I discovered there are constants that never change, a solid foundation for my life; God the Father, Jesus Christ, the Holy Spirit, and the Word of God. They are always with me, leading and guiding me.

In this book you will learn more about Jesus

and the importance he can play in your life. I pray that as you read this book, God will give you revelation of who Jesus is and what he did for you by dying on the cross to pay for your sins.

I remember three times in my life when I should have died but God had mercy on me. I owe my life to Jesus for what he has done for me, so now I live to please him.

The first time I almost died is when I was working offshore on an oilfield pipeline barge. We were working in twelve-to fifteen-foot seas. Our work station was about three feet above sea level. After the pipe was welded, we sealed the pipes with a hot tar mix before sending it into the ocean. At one point a fifteen-foot wave hit me and pulled me overboard. I was wearing a blue denim shirt, denim jeans, and heavy-duty work boots. I was disoriented and began sinking. I felt someone grab me by the hand and pull me to the barge where a ladder was located. I looked around but saw no one. I was able to climb to safety. It was God's angel protecting me.

Another time when I was in college, I went home for the weekend. I had a sinus infection and was taking antibiotics. Even though I did not feel well, I went out for a couple of drinks. After I drank one beer, I decided to drive home. I fell asleep going around sixty miles per hour and hit a ditch culvert head-on without wearing a seat belt. I totaled my father's truck that night, but to my amazement, I walked away unharmed. Again God's guardian angel was protecting me.

The next time I should have died, I was driving around ninety-five miles per hour on the interstate heading toward Denver, Colorado. It was snowing, visibility was low, and again I was not wearing my seat belt. This was a combination for disaster. I approached a sharp curve and went airborne, landing in a concrete canal. I felt someone restrain me before impact; it was my guardian angel. I walked away with just three fractured ribs. God spared me because my destiny had not yet been fulfilled.

I know God has a purpose and a plan for my life. He inspired me to write this book so that many would be spared from eternal death and come to know Jesus Christ as their Lord and Savior.

Chapter 1

God's Creation

I am sure you have heard different theories about how the earth was formed, as well as people. I will give you a biblical account of how God created all things in Genesis 1.

In the beginning, before God created everything, Jesus existed with him. Jesus is the visible image of the invisible God and is supreme over all creation. Jesus is the one through whom God created everything in heaven and earth. He made the things we can see and the things we can't see. Everything has been created through him and for him. He existed before everything else began, and he holds all creation together (Colossians 1:16–17 NLT).

God created the greater light (sun) for day and the lesser light (moon) for night. He set borders from the sea and dry land. He spoke into existence all the fish and creatures of the sea. On the land, he created all seed-bearing plants and fruit trees. God spoke, and the earth brought forth every kind of animal: livestock, small animals, and wildlife (Genesis 1 NLT).

Then God said,

> Let us make people in our image, to be like ourselves. They will be masters over all life—the fish in the sea, the birds in the sky, and all livestock, wild animals, and small animals. God patterned them after himself; male and female he created them. (Genesis 1:26–27 NLT)

God gave the man and the woman a body, a soul, and a spirit. Your body is physical in nature but will eventually will die. The soul is comprised of your mind, will, and emotions. Your soul will live forever, unlike your body. You are also given a spirit that gives life to your body. Your spirit will also live forever.

The Fall of Adam and Eve

God planted a garden for Adam and Eve so that they could tend and eat its fruit. God also planted in the middle of the garden the tree of life and the tree of the knowledge of good and evil. God gave them strict instructions not to eat from this tree or they would surely die.

Satan, the tempter, was in the garden with Adam and Eve. One day he tempted Eve to eat fruit from the forbidden tree. It looked pleasing to Eve; she fell for the trap and ate the fruit. She gave some to Adam, and they both soon realized they were naked. They were ashamed of what they did and afraid of what God would do to them because of this sin of disobedience. As punishment, God banished them from the garden. Sin cannot coexist with God and go unpunished. Adam relinquished his authority over the earth to Satan.

Chapter 2

God's Redemptive Plan

Since Adam and Eve had sinned, they were cast out of the Garden of Eden. They had to provide for themselves. God now required a blood sacrifice to atone for sin. For generation after generation, God required a spotless lamb be sacrificed.

At the right time, God made known his plan of salvation and his perfect atonement for all of humankind's sin. He sent his Son, Jesus, into the world to experience life with the trials and tribulations we all face. Jesus was sinless but became sin to conquer it. By his shed blood on the cross, Jesus accomplished his mission

- to destroy the works of Satan
- to take back the authority Satan stole from Adam and give it back to believers of Jesus Christ
- to save sinners
- to provide a way for salvation
- to restore our fellowship with God

Satan's job is to kill, steal, and destroy. He wants to kill your dreams, steal your soul, and destroy your life.

Jesus came so that we may have eternal life and live more abundantly.

Humankind needed a mediator to restore communication and relationship with God. Jesus is your mediator and intercedes for you. Jesus is the Lamb of God who takes away the sins of the world. He was the perfect offering as a sacrifice for our sins, once and for all. You no longer need to have sacrifices to pay for your sins. Jesus did it for you.

Chapter 3

Names of Jesus

The names of Jesus reflect his character, his authority, and his power. Below are twenty-three names of Jesus mentioned in the Bible.

Advocate

An advocate is one who pleads another's case. If you sin, there is someone to plead for you before the Father. He is Jesus Christ, the one who pleases God completely. He is the perfect sacrifice for our sins (1 John 2:1–2 NLT).

If you sin, you can claim the promise of 1 John 1:9 (NLT), which says, "If we confess our sins, he is faithful and just and will forgive us our sins and purify us from all unrighteousness." As far as the east is from the west, God remembers your sins no more. If God does not remember your sins, then you should not dwell on them. Rejoice that your sins have been forgiven. Remember you must also forgive yourself and go on with your life. The enemy will try to make you feel guilty and try to condemn you. All who belong to Christ are free from guilt and condemnation.

Lamb of God

John the Baptist saw Jesus coming toward him and said, "Look! There is the Lamb of God who takes away the sins of the world" (John 1:29 NLT).

In the Old Testament, God commanded the Israelite priests to offer sacrificial lambs, ones without blemishes, for the sins of the people. Without the blood sacrifices, there was no forgiveness of sins. Lambs had to be sacrificed to atone for the sins of Israel, but this was not a permanent solution.

In the New Testament, God provided the perfect sacrifice for the sins of all people: his Son, Jesus Christ, the Lamb of God. All who call on his name and ask for forgiveness of their sins will be cleansed of all unrighteousness, and their sins will no longer be held against them.

The Resurrection and the Life

Jesus was crucified and died a physical death on the cross, but death could not hold him. He descended into hell and took back the authority Satan had taken from Adam.

Jesus rose on the third day from the grave and appeared before Mary, Martha, and his disciples. Jesus ascended into heaven to be glorified with the Father. He came back to meet with his disciples with further instructions. He breathed on them, and they were filled with the Holy Spirit. He told them to go out and preach the gospel and heal the sick. Jesus came to earth from time to time as a witness to the believers.

Now he is seated at the right hand of God. His work on earth is finished. Jesus said:

> I am the Resurrection and the Life. Those who believe in me, even though they die like everyone else, will live again. They are

given eternal life for believing in me and will never perish. (John 11:25–26 NLT)

Shepherd and Bishop of Souls

A shepherd is one who tends and cares for his sheep. Jesus is the good shepherd who looks after his sheep. All believers are considered his sheep, and he will not lose any.

Jesus is the bishop of souls, our guardian and overseer. For you were as sheep going astray, but now you are returned to the shepherd and bishop of your souls (1 Peter 2:25 NLT).

Judge

Jesus is the just judge whose judgments are perfect and pure. He will judge the world—both the living and the dead. God left all judgment to his Son, Jesus. And he ordered us to preach everywhere and to testify that Jesus is ordained of God to be judge of all—the living and the dead (Acts 10:42 NLT). You will be judged on your acceptance or rejection of Jesus Christ as your Lord and Savior.

The final judgment is described in scripture:

> But when the Son of man comes in his glory, and all the angels with him, then he will sit upon his glorious throne. All the nations will be gathered in his presence, and he will separate them as a shepherd separates the sheep from the goats (the sheep represent the believers and the goats represent the unbelievers). He will place the sheep at his right hand and the goats at his left. Then the King will say to those on the right, "Come you who are blessed by my Father inherit the Kingdom prepared for you from the foundation of the world." (Matthew 25:31–34 NLT)

Then the king will turn to those on the left and say, "Away with you, you cursed ones, into the eternal fire prepared for the Devil and his demons" (Matthew 25:41 NLT).

The righteous ones will be rewarded by Jesus based on how they lived and the good deeds they performed. Your reward awaits you in heaven!

King of Kings and Lord of Lords

Jesus is lord and king. Lord is someone having power and authority. King means sovereign and ruler. Jesus has the authority and the power to rule and reign over all the earth.

In the end, Jesus will be supreme ruler, having defeated and conquered all other rulers. He will establish his reign over all the earth.

So that at the name of Jesus, every knee will bow both in heaven and on earth and under the earth, and every tongue will confess that Jesus Christ is Lord, to the glory of God the Father (Philippians 2:10–11 NLT).

For at the right time, Christ will be revealed from heaven by the blessed and only almighty God, the king of kings and lord of lords (1 Timothy 6:15 NLT).

Man of Sorrows

He was despised and rejected—a man of sorrows acquainted with bitterest grief. We turned our backs on him and looked the other way when he went by. He was despised, and we did not care (Isaiah 53:3 NLT).

Isaiah prophesied about Jesus and the sorrows and grief he would suffer. Jesus lived on the earth as a man in the flesh. The Jewish leaders despised and ridiculed him. He was mocked and laughed at. They had him beaten and crucified. Although Jesus was innocent of all charges against him, he did not defend himself or call on angels to rescue him. He endured the crucifixion and suffering on the cross.

The religious leaders rejected Jesus with cold hearts not knowing he was the Messiah. Jesus grieved for the lost souls he came to save. Even Jesus's disciples abandoned him when he needed them the most. Jesus had compassion for the Jews, but they had no compassion toward him.

Head of the Church

Christ is the head of his body, the church; he gave his life to be her savior. Jesus is the leader of the church and the church should follow him. Jesus directs and governs his people toward their destiny and purpose. And God has put all things under the authority of Christ, and he gave him this authority for the benefit of the Church. The Church is his body; it is filled by Christ, who fills everything everywhere with his presence (Ephesians 1:22–23 NLT).

The believer is to become more in everything like Christ. Under his direction, the whole body is fitted together perfectly. As each part does its own special work, it helps the other parts grow, so that the whole body is healthy and growing and full of love.

The Lord Jesus Christ built the Church, and the gates of hell will not prevail. We are to conquer and take ground for the kingdom of God.

Master

Master is defined in *The Merriam-Webster Dictionary* as one who has authority or control. Jesus taught with great authority. He cast out demons, healed the sick, raised the dead, and performed many miracles.

One day Jesus said to his disciples, "Let's cross over to the other side of the lake." So they got into a boat and started out. On the way across, Jesus lay down for a nap, and while he was sleeping the wind began to rise. A fierce storm developed that threatened to swamp them, and they were in real danger.

The disciples woke him up, shouting, "Master, Master, we're going to drown!"

Jesus rebuked the wind and the raging waves. The storm stopped, and all was calm! (Luke 8:22–24 NLT). Jesus is master of all, even the wind and sea.

He is master over all believers. His commands are just and true. Paul claimed to be a slave to Jesus Christ. We are to adhere to the Word of God and carry out his will.

Faithful and True Witness

Jesus is called the faithful and true witness in Revelation. Jesus is faithful to God in all he says and does. Since Jesus was with God before creation of the world, he is the true witness of God—his character, authority, and power. Jesus represented God here on earth.

Jesus wants you to be faithful to God and be a witness for him.

Jesus warns us not to be addicted to the ways of the world. He hates a lukewarm Christian. He prefers you to be hot and passionate to the ways of God, putting Christ first in your life.

His judgment is near. Will you be included when Jesus calls his church to meet him with his army, or will you be left behind to face Satan and his demons?

Jesus is the one who corrects and disciplines those he loves.

Jesus desires that you be faithful to him and a witness for him by your testimony of what he did for you.

Rock

Jesus is the rock, a solid foundation for your life. The Lord is my rock, my fortress, and my savior; my God is my rock, in whom I find protection. He is my shield, the strength of my salvation, and my stronghold (Psalm 18:2 NLT).

In the Old Testament, Jesus was the miraculous rock that traveled with the Israelites in the wildness. And all of them drank miraculous water from the rock.

Jesus is the rock on which to build your foundation of faith. Jesus is the same yesterday, today, and forever. You can always trust him; he is tried and true from generation to generation. He will place your feet on the rock of solid ground. You can stand firm on the Word of God. Let Jesus be the rock in your life. He will keep you sturdy on the path to salvation and righteousness.

High Priest

Jesus is your high priest who intercedes for you with God the Father. He is holy, set apart for the service of high priest. He offered himself as the sacrifice for your sins and to cleanse you from all unrighteousness. You can approach Jesus, the high priest, and confess your sins.

You can come to Jesus for refuge and take new courage for you can hold onto his promises with confidence. This confidence is like a strong and trustworthy anchor for your soul. It leads you through the curtain of heaven into God's sanctuary. Jesus has already gone there for you. He has become your eternal high priest (Hebrews 6:18–19 NLT). You can go directly to Jesus, your high priest, to confess your sins. He stands before God waiting to acquit you of all your sins. He directs your path to righteousness and holy living.

The Door

Jesus is the door to salvation. "I am the door. If anyone enters me, he will be saved" (John 10:9 NKJV). Jesus is the only door to heaven; there are no other ways. Those who are saved can go through the door. The door awaits your entrance.

Are you willing to accept Jesus Christ as

your Lord and Savior? If you said yes, you will have the key to the door. "Behold, I stand at the door and knock. If anyone hears my voice and opens the door, I will come into him and dine with him, and he with me" (Revelation 3:20 NKJV).

Living Water

Jesus is the living water. Jesus said to the Samaritan woman at the well, "If you only know the gift God has for you and who I am, you would ask me, and I would give you living water" (John 4:9–10 NLT).

Jesus was talking about the Holy Spirit. Jesus wants you to have the Holy Spirit dwelling in you to lead, guide, and teach you the ways of God.

On the last day, the climax of the festival, Jesus stood and shouted to the crowds, "Anyone who is thirsty may come to me! Anyone who believes in me may come and drink! For the Scriptures declare, rivers of living water will flow from the heart" (John 7:37–39 NLT). Jesus again was speaking of being filled with the Holy Spirit.

Jesus said, "People soon become thirsty after drinking this water. But the water I give them takes away thirst altogether. It becomes a perpetual spring within them, giving them eternal life" (John 4:13 NLT).

Do you have the Holy Spirit living in you? If not, ask Jesus to save you and fill you with the Holy Spirit.

The Bread of Life

Jesus is the bread of life. In Jesus's time, bread was a main food staple. One could live on bread and water for a long time.

Since Jesus is the bread of life, all who come to him will never hunger spiritually. Jesus is the needed nourishment for your soul. He gives you eternal life.

Without the bread of life, you are spiritually dead. You don't have any chance of going to heaven.

In the Old Testament, Moses led the children of Israel out of bondage in Egypt toward the land God promised the Israelites. Even though they had seen God do great miracles for them—delivered them from Pharaoh, safety from the plagues in Egypt, prosperity of their livestock while Egypt lost all their livestock and crops and firstborn children, parting of the Red Sea to bring them to safety from Pharaoh and his army who were destroyed in the Red Sea—they still could not believe God would provide food for them in the wilderness. God was trying to teach these doubters that he would in fact provide for them. So God rained down manna from heaven for them to eat. Manna is the bread from heaven, the food of angels.

Jesus is the manna, the substance of eternal life; partake in him.

Alpha and Omega

Jesus is the alpha and omega; the beginning and the end. Alpha and omega are the first and the last letters of the Greek alphabet. Jesus is found in Genesis and Revelation, the beginning and the end of the Bible. Jesus always was and always will be. He existed before creation and will always be eternal.

He was in the beginning with God. He created everything there is. Nothing exists that he didn't make. Life itself was in him, and this life gives light to everyone (John 1:2–4 NLT).

Jesus said, "See, I am coming soon, and my reward is with me, to repay all according to their deeds. I am the Alpha and the Omega, the First and the Last, the Beginning and the End" (Revelation 22:12–13 NLT).

Jesus is the author and finisher of our faith. When you get saved, Jesus imparts a measure of faith in you. Jesus will help you grow in faith through circumstances and trails. Jesus is faithful and is always there to pick you up when you fall. His plan is to bring you into maturity of faith, so you will lack nothing. You only need a little faith for God to move on your behalf.

True Vine

Jesus is the true vine. Jesus said,

> I am the true vine, and my Father
> is the gardener. He cuts off every

branch that doesn't produce fruit, and he prunes the branches that do bear fruit so they will produce even more. You have already been pruned for greater fruitfulness by the message I have given you. Remain in me, and I will remain in you. For a branch cannot produce fruit if it is severed from the Vine, and you cannot be fruitful apart from me. Yes I am the Vine; you are the branches. Those who remain in me, and I in them, will produce much fruit. For apart from me you can do nothing. (John 15:1–5 NLT)

The kind of fruit Jesus was talking about is: love, joy, peace, goodness, kindness, gentleness, faithfulness, and self-control.

Without Jesus, you are cut off from the vine of eternal life. Stay plugged into Jesus, and he will direct your life into blessings and fruitfulness.

Messiah

*To simplify things, I will distinguish Old Testament prophesies with the abbreviation OT. I will present New Testament fulfillments with the abbreviation NT.

Jesus is the Messiah, meaning the anointed one. The Jewish people had their hopes up that their Messiah would be an earthly king and would deliver them from foreign rulers. They did not recognize him as the heavenly king who was a humble servant.

Isaiah prophesied, "For a child is born to us, a Son is given to us. And the government will rest on his shoulders. These will be his royal titles: Wonderful, Counselor, Mighty God, Everlasting Father, and Prince of Peace. His ever expanding, peaceful government will never end. He will rule forever with fairness and justice from the throne of his ancestor David" (Isaiah 9:6–7 NLT).

Other prophesies about the Messiah:

- OT: The Messiah would be born of a virgin in Bethlehem.

  o "But you, O Bethlehem, are only a small village in Judah. Yet a ruler of Israel will come from you, one whose origins are from distant past. The people of Israel will be abandoned to their enemies until the time when the woman in labor gives birth to her Son. Then at last his fellow countrymen will return from exile to their own land. And he will stand to lead his flock with the Lord's strength in the majesty of the name of the Lord his God" (Micah 5:2–4 NLT).

- NT: Jesus was born in Bethlehem.

  o We in see in Matthew chapter 2 that Joseph and Mary had to travel to Bethlehem to register for the census, while in Bethlehem, Mary gave birth to Jesus, the Messiah.

- OT: They would gamble for his clothing.

  o "They divide my clothes among themselves and throw dice for my garments" (Psalm 22:18 NLT).

- NT: The soldiers gambled for his clothes

  o This was fulfilled in Matthew 27:35 (NLT). After they had nailed him to the cross, the soldiers gambled for his clothes by throwing dice.

- OT: His ancestry would be from the tribe of Judah.

  o "The scepter will not depart from Judah, nor the rulers staff from his descendants, until the coming of the one to whom it belongs, the one whom all nations will obey" (Genesis 49:10 NLT).

- NT: Jesus came from the tribe of Judah

  o In Matthew chapter 1, Jesus came from the lineage of King David, who was from the tribe of Judah.

- OT: He was declared by God to be his Son.

  o "The King proclaims the Lords decree: 'The Lord said to me, you are my Son. Today I have become your Father'" (Psalm 2:7 NLT).

- NT: God declares Jesus to be his Son.

  o "After Jesus was baptized by John the Baptist, a voice from heaven said, 'This is my beloved son, and I am fully pleased with him'" (Matthew 3:17 NLT).

- OT: The Messiah would bring in a new covenant.

  o "'The day will come,' says the Lord, 'When I will make a new covenant with the people of Israel and Judah. This covenant will not be like the one I made with their ancestors when I took them by the hand and brought them out of the land of Egypt. They broke that covenant, though I loved them as a husband loves his wife,' says the Lord" (Jeremiah 31:31 NLT).

- NT: Jesus makes a new covenant.

  o "But this new covenant I will make with the people of Israel on that day," says the Lord, "I will put my laws in their minds, and I will write them on their hearts. I will be their God, and they will be my people" (Hebrews 8:10 NLT). The new covenant between God and you is sealed by the shedding of Jesus's blood.

- OT: The Messiah would not be accepted by his own people.

  o "He was despised and rejected—a man of sorrows, acquainted with bitterest grief. We turned our backs on him and looked the other way when he went by. He was despised and we did not care" (Isaiah 53:3 NLT).

- NT: Jesus was rejected.

  o "Even in his own land and among his people, he was not accepted" (John 1:11 NLT).

- OT: The Messiah would be raised from the dead.

  o "But as for me, God will redeem my life. He will snatch me from the power of death" (Psalm 49:15 NLT).

- NT: Jesus was raised from the dead.

  o Mary Magdalene and the other Mary went out to see Jesus's tomb. Then the angel spoke to the women and said, "I know you are looking for Jesus, who was crucified. He isn't here! He has been raised from the dead, just as he said would happen" (Matthew 28:5–6 NLT).

- OT: The Messiah would suffer for our sins.

  o "He was wounded and crushed for our sins. He was beaten so we might have peace. He was whipped and we were healed!" (Isaiah 53:5). "Yet the Lord laid on him the guilt and sins of us all" (Isaiah 53:6).

- NT: Jesus suffered and died for our sins.

  o "You rejected this holy, righteous one and instead demanded the release of a murderer. You killed the author of life, but God raised him to life" (Acts 3:14–15 NLT). "What you did to Jesus was done in ignorance. But God was fulfilling what all the prophets had declared about the Messiah beforehand—that he must suffer all these things" (Acts 3:17–18 NLT).

- NT: Jesus fulfilled the law and the prophets.

  o "Jesus took Peter and the two brothers, James and John, and led them up a high mountain. As the men watched, Jesus's appearance changed so that his face shone like the sun, and his clothing became dazzling white. Suddenly, Moses and Elijah appeared and began talking with Jesus" (Matthew 17:1–3 NLT). Moses represented the law because he wrote the law. Elijah was a great prophet, so he represented the prophets. Jesus fulfilled both the law and the prophecies written about him.

Teacher

Jesus was a miraculous teacher. A Pharisee came to speak with Jesus. "Teacher," he said, "we all know that God has sent you to teach us. Your miraculous signs are proof enough that God is with you" (John 3:2 NLT).

Jesus taught with authority. After Jesus

finished speaking, the crowds were amazed at his teaching, for he taught as one who had real authority—quite unlike the teachers of religious law (Matthew 7:28–29 NLT).

Jesus showed his authority by healing the sick and casting out demons. Jesus healed a man with leprosy. A man with leprosy approached Jesus. He knelt before him, worshipping. "Lord," said the man, "if you want to, you can make me well again." Jesus touched him. "I want to," he said. "Be healed!" And instantly the leprosy disappeared (Matthew 8:2–3 NLT).

Jesus healed many people. Jesus went to Peter's house. Peter's mother-in-law was sick in bed with high fever. Jesus touched her hand, the fever left her. That evening many demon-possessed people were brought to Jesus. All the evil spirits fled when he commanded them to leave, and he healed all the sick (Matthew 8:16 NLT).

Mediator

A mediator is a negotiator between parties who acts as a go-between to resolve an issue.

Jesus is your mediator. For there is only one God and one mediator who can reconcile God and people; he is the man Christ Jesus. He gave his life to purchase freedom for everyone (1 Timothy 2:5–6 NLT).

For by the power of the eternal Spirit, Christ offered himself to God as a perfect sacrifice for our sins. That is why he is the one who mediates the new covenant between God and people, so that all who are invited can receive the eternal inheritance God has promised them. For Christ died to set them free from the penalty of the sins they had committed under the first covenant (Hebrews 9:14–15 NLT).

You have come to Jesus, the one who mediates the new covenant between God and people (Hebrews 12:24 NLT).

Accept Jesus Christ as you Lord and Savior, so he can be your mediator.

Jesus Is the Light of the World

Jesus said to the people, "I am the light of the world. If you follow me, you won't be stumbling through the darkness, because you will have the light that leads to life" (John 8:12 NLT).

As God's children, Jesus said, "You are the light of the world—like a city on a mountain, glowing in the night for all to see. Don't hide your light! Instead let it shine for all. In the same way, let your good deeds shine out for all to see, so that everyone will praise your heavenly Father" (Matthew 5:14–18 NLT).

The psalmist said in Psalm 27:1 (NLT), "The Lord is my light and my salvation."

Jesus Christ in all his glory is the light that shines in the darkness. He is the visible image of the invisible God.

Jesus Christ Is Lord

You may have heard the saying, "Jesus is Lord." What does that mean? In Hebrew the name Jesus means God saves. Jesus is our Savior.

Christ means the anointed one. He was anointed by God to save sinners and bring God's Word into reality. He healed the sick, the blind, and raised the dead. He taught with authority, and even the demons obeyed his command.

Jesus was given all authority in heaven and on earth by almighty God.

Lord means a person with great power and authority. Jesus Christ is the Son of God. He was resurrected from the dead. He was given authority to rule and reign over the earth and to judge the living and the dead.

Jesus's name should be honored and revered as holy and treated with upmost respect.

Jesus—The Word of God

In the beginning, the Word already existed. He was with God, and he was God (John 1:1 NLT).

The Word became human and lived here on earth among us. He was full of unfailing love and faithfulness. And we have seen his glory, the glory of the only Son of the Father (John 1:14 NLT).

The Word of God is full of living power. It is sharper than the sharpest knife, cutting deep into our innermost thoughts and desires. It exposes us for what we really are. Nothing in all creation can hide from him (Hebrews 4:12 NLT).

The Word gives life to your soul and meaning to your life. The Word convicts us of our sins but also leads us to repentance.

The Word is health to our bodies. He sent his Word and healed them (Psalm 107:20 KJV).

Reading the Bible breathes new life with joy and hope when you study and apply the Word to your life. It will change you forever.

Chapter 4

Jesus the Healer

Jesus was sent down from heaven as the Son of God to save sinners. He demonstrated his love by healing the sick and brokenhearted. Jesus took our sickness and removed our diseases (Matthew 8:7 NLT). Everywhere Jesus went he healed the sick and cast out demons. Jesus's healing power is demonstrated in the gospels of Matthew, Mark, Luke, and John. Jesus healed a leper in Galilee. He healed a Roman Centurion's servant. Jesus healed Peter's mother-in-law and many others who were at her home. Jesus also healed paralyzed people. Jesus healed in response to faith. He healed the deaf and the blind. Jesus healed the demon-possessed daughter of a gentile woman who had faith.

There are many other examples of Jesus's

healing in the Bible. Healing scriptures in the Bible are for you. Here are some listed:

1. "He sent his Word and healed them" (Psalm 107:20 KJV).
2. "Praise the Lord, O my soul and forget not all his benefits—who forgives all your sins and heals all your diseases" (Psalm 103:2–3 KJV).
3. "The prayers offered in faith will heal the sick" (James 5:15 NLT).
4. "You have been healed by his wounds" (1 Peter 2:24 NLT).
5. "He heals the broken-hearted, binding up their wounds" (Psalm 147:3 NLT).
6. "'I will give you back your health and heal your wounds,' says the Lord" (Jeremiah 30:17 NLT).
7. "A cheerful heart is good medicine" (Proverbs 17:22 NLT).
8. "Lord your discipline is good, for it leads to life and health. You restore my health and allow me to live" (Isaiah 38:16 NLT).
9. "Confess your sins to each other and pray for each other so that you may be healed. The earnest prayer of a righteous person

has great power and wonderful results" (James 5:16 NLT).

10. "He took our sickness and removed our diseases" (Matthew 8:17 NLT).

The Word of God is health to a person's whole body. Confess the Word of God over your health. God is a rewarder of those who seek him.

I am a personal witness to Jesus Christ's healing. I came from an alcoholic family. I struggled with alcohol for a while. Someone prayed with me, and Jesus took away that desire.

I went through three divorces over which I suffered emotional and psychological pain. I had low self-esteem. I felt like my life did not amount to much, but Jesus came in and traded his beauty for my ashes. He healed me from the emotional and psychological pain. He breathed new life into me with purpose and meaning. I am at the happiest stage of my life. God is not through with me. I have my God-given destiny to fulfill.

Jesus did it for me, and he can heal you too. Have faith in God and believe Jesus can and will heal you.

Jesus said, "Ask, using my name, and you will receive, and you will have abundant joy" (John 16:24 NLT). You can come bodily to the throne of grace and ask what you need with thanksgiving. Jesus gave you a legal right to use his name for your healing—physical, mental, and emotional.

When you follow Jesus Christ and obey his commands, God's blessings will follow you.

Chapter 5

Jesus the Savior

There is no other way to receive salvation and go to heaven but through Jesus Christ. God in his wisdom set in motion his plan and will for us to be a part of heaven.

God did not make us robots to worship him. We are made human with flesh and blood, with a mind, will, and emotions. He made us in three parts: body, soul, and spirit.

Your body is meant to be a temple of the Holy Spirit to house the Spirit of God. God has numbered our days here on earth and then the afterlife. What you do here on earth will determine where you will spend eternity. God purposed your life to spend eternity with him in heaven; however, he has given you a free will to do as you please. You can choose to live a godly life, led by the Holy Spirit, or a life according to the evil desires of you flesh. That choice is yours.

God has also given you a soul to live in your body. Your soul is your mind, your will, and your emotions.

He has given you a mind so that you can think and reason things out. His desire is for you to have your mind set on him and his Son, Jesus.

Jesus knew his purpose and meaning here on earth. When Jesus came down from heaven in the flesh, God's Spirit was upon him without measure or limit. The Father loves his Son and has given him authority over everything. And all who believe in God's son have eternal life (John 4:34–36 NLT).

Jesus ministered love and compassion among his people. He instructed them on God's truths. He healed the sick, the lame, the blind, and cast out demons. Jesus was obedient to God even obedient to lay down his life on the cross.

Jesus left an inheritance of salvation when he died on the cross. An inheritance of forgiveness for your sins and eternal salvation. An inheritance is not claimed until a person dies.

As a believer of Jesus Christ, you will inherit the kingdom of heaven when your body dies. To be absent from the body is to be present with the Lord (2 Corinthians 5:8 KJV).

God has given you a free will. You have the ability to choose right or wrong, eternal life or eternal death. You might say, "Well, I don't believe in that." If you don't, then Satan will make that decision for you. Satan has blinded the minds of unbelievers so they will not know the truth of the saving power of the gospel of Jesus Christ.

God wants you to worship him for who he is. On the other hand, Satan would like for you to worship him. Satan's purpose is to steal your soul, kill your dreams, and destroy your life.

Jesus's purpose is to give you life in all its fullness (John 10:10 NLT). Jesus laid down his life for you so that you can have your sins forgiven and live a blessed life here on earth and spend eternity with him in heaven.

God gave you emotions. What a dull life it would be if you had no emotions. Your emotions should be directed toward God. There is a season to be happy and laugh, to feel sorrow and pain, and to grieve at the loss of a loved one.

God wants you to keep your emotions under control. You should not be stuck in a state of sorrow, pain, and grief. You should have joy in the good times as well as the bad. The prospect of the righteous is joy, but the hopes of the wicked come to nothing (Proverbs 10:28 NIV). Weeping may go on all night, but joy comes with the morning (Psalm 30:5 NLT).

The Bible instructs you to put the kingdom of God as a high priority in your life. For the kingdom of God is righteousness, peace, and joy in the Holy Spirit (Romans 14:17 NIV).

Jesus is worthy of your praise because of what he did for you. You should praise him with great emotion.

Your body is also made of spirit. God breathed spirit into you so that your body would live. One day your body will die, but your soul (mind, will, and emotions) and spirit will live forever.

God has given you a choice of what kind of spirit to have. Will it be a spirit that leads to eternal life, or will it be a spirit that leads to eternal death?

When you receive salvation from Jesus Christ, the Holy Spirit resides in you. You will go on to be with the Lord in heaven. When a person does not believe in Jesus and rejects his salvation, he will spend eternity in hell where there is darkness, torment, and great suffering.

God's Holy Spirit will lead and guide you. He is there to comfort you, teach you the ways of the Lord, and warn you of danger or making bad decisions.

On the other hand, a person without the Holy Spirit will be led by Satan on a path of worldliness, sin, and destruction. Satan blinds the eyes and minds of the unbeliever so that person thinks he does not need God. The wages of sin is (eternal) death, but the gift of God is eternal life through Christ Jesus our Lord (Romans 6:23 NLT). Will you be led by the Holy Spirit or an evil spirit? You will have to give an account to God on that matter.

In the name of Jesus there is forgiveness from you sins. Everyone who believes in him is freed from all guilt and declared right with God (Acts 13:16 NLT). For God so loved the world that he gave his only Son, so that everyone who believes in him will not perish but have eternal life (John 3:16 NLT). And all who believe in God's Son have eternal life (John 3:36 NLT).

For we are God's masterpiece. He has created us anew in Christ Jesus so that we can do the good deeds he planned for us long ago (Ephesians 2:10 NLT).

God made you for a purpose: to live according to his Word, to serve others, and follow Jesus's commands.

Chapter 6

Things to Know about Jesus

1. Jesus is a real person, history tells us so; our time is measured in BC (before Christ) and AD, which is Latin for "anno domini," meaning in the year of our Lord.

2. Jesus loves you so much that he died to save you and forgive your sins.

3. Jesus is the only way to heaven.

4. Jesus bore our sickness and diseases.

5. Jesus reconciled us to God the Father.

6. Jesus volunteered to come down from heaven in human form. He went through unfair judgments, beatings, and crucifixion on the cross. He faced life with the same trails, tribulations, and

temptations that we all go through, yet he did not sin.

7. Jesus defeated Satan and gave us back the authority over the earth that Adam once had.

8. Jesus is Lord over every ruler and has authority over the earth. There is no other name above the name of Jesus.

9. Jesus took all your sins upon his cross, and you are set free from the power of the devil and his forces of evil.

10. Jesus is coming back to judge the living and the dead.

11. Jesus has given you authority to use his name to defeat Satan and overcome your circumstances.

12. Jesus is coming back for you. Are you ready?

13. Jesus desires to be a part of your life.

14. Jesus is Lord and Savior.

> Have you received Jesus as your Lord and Savior? If you want him as Lord, you can say this simple prayer: "Lord Jesus, I come to you a sinner. I ask you to come into my heart and forgive me my sins. I repent of my sins, and

I will follow you for the rest of my life." Friend, if you said this prayer and meant it, I believe your spirit is reborn. Get a Bible and go to a Bible-based church where you can be taught the Word of God.

1. You have victory in Jesus Christ.
2. Jesus loves to forgive you of your sins, not condemn you.
3. Jesus welcomes you to his throne of grace.
4. Jesus is always accessible.
5. Jesus set you free from the slavery of sin.
6. Jesus is God's Son. He was with God in the beginning when the universe was created.
7. Jesus is the word of life. All scripture is inspired by God and is useful to teach us what is true and to make us realize what is wrong in our lives. It straightens us out and teaches us to do what is right. It is God's way of preparing us in every way, fully equipped for every good thing God wants us to do (2 Timothy 3:16–17 NLT).
8. Jesus is coming back again to receive his bride—the church (all who are saved). He will conquer death once and for all! He

will rule and reign in the New Jerusalem forever and ever!

In Jesus, you have power, you have peace, you have love, you have joy, you have hope, you have purpose, and you have eternal life.

Chapter 7

Guilt and Condemnation

I have struggled with guilt and condemnation for most of my life. When I made mistakes, I would dwell on what I did wrong and play it over and over in my mind. It was like a record on an endless loop saying, "You are a failure, you are a failure, you are a failure." I had a negative outlook on life because I dwelt on the past and did not envision a better life ahead of me. The Bible tells us whatever you think about, you will become. If you think failure, chances are you will fail. If you think of yourself as inferior, then you will probably develop a mind-set that you are not good enough. I struggled with this a lot. I had thought for so long about my failures instead of my victories that it became a stronghold in my life.

The Bible says you are to renew your mind. What does this mean? It means to read and study God's Word and thank him for his goodness. You are to think the way God wants you to think. God is love, so you are to receive his love and give love to others.

Since I had such a stronghold on my negative thought life, it took me a long time to forgive myself and move on. Have I reached perfection in this area? No, I still have to determine in my mind that I am a victor and not a victim. I must think positively on purpose. I must delete negative thoughts that come my way. The scripture tells us to take every thought captive to the obedience of Jesus Christ. You are to dispel wrong thinking and replace it with right thinking that is based on the Word of God.

The devil will send negative thoughts your way to make you feel guilt and condemnation. It is your job to repel such thoughts and replace them with positive thoughts and positive affirmations. I find it helpful to read the Bible and other inspiring books that are positive and give you hope. Your hope should be based on what Jesus did for you on the cross. Your future is in heaven – dwell on that. Know that God has a purpose and plan for your life and a bright future.

There is no condemnation for those who belong to Jesus Christ. Condemnation does not come from God, it is of the devil. He likes to beat you up and tear you down to inferior thinking. He wants you to be consumed with dwelling on yourself. When you think of others, do what is good, and love others, you won't have time to think about your faults.

I have found it helpful to listen to positive and inspirational preaching from Joel Osteen and Joyce Meyer.

Develop a plan to counterattack negative thoughts. Your enemy is trying to defeat you in your thought life. Your mind is a battlefield. You must be prepared to battle the enemy with the Word of God and positive affirmations of who you are in Christ Jesus. Your future depends on it. Victories are won or lost in your mind. You have to think victory before your get the victory. If you think defeat, then you will be defeated.

You will find in life that you move toward what you are thinking about. Success doesn't just happen on its own. You have to think positively about your future to bring about your success.

Get over hurt feelings and disappointments from your past. They are a stumbling block for your future. The apostle Paul said it best:

> I am focusing all my energies on this one thing. Forgetting the past and looking forward to what lies ahead. I strain to reach the end of the race and receive the prize for which God, through Christ Jesus is calling us up to heaven. (Philippians 3:13–14 NLT)

Forget your past mistakes and move on with your life. Remember, you belong to Jesus Christ, so don't allow guilt or condemnation in your thought life. Guilt and condemnation comes from Satan, and there is no condemnation for those who belong to Jesus. Instead think about God's favor in your life. God's goodness and mercy are flowing your way. God's blessings are chasing you down. Expect circumstances to change in your favor.

Chapter 8

The Effects of Sin in Your Life

Sin is an immoral act considered to be a transgression against God. Sin has many consequences:

- Separates you from fellowship with God
- Leaves you with guilt and condemnation
- Gives the devil an open door to your life
- Pushes you away from dependence on God
- Causes you to lose your joy, peace, and confidence
- You become fearful of the consequences
- Shuts off God's blessings
- Becomes a curse in your life
- Your prayers will not be answered
- Defiles a person's conscience and soul

- Everyone who commits sin is a slave to sin
- Destroys relationships
- Life becomes meaningless to the sinner
- Is a disgrace to anyone who sins
- Sin will take you farther than you want to go
- Sin will cost you more than you want to pay
- Sin will keep you longer than you want to stay
- Pride is a sin. Pride is a consuming desire of selfishness. It sees other people, all of creation, money, and things to use in service to one's selfishness. The recipe to kill pride is humility. Humble yourself before the Lord, and he will lift you up (James 4:10 NIV).
- Sexual immorality is a sin. It has been known to destroy individuals as well as nations. We see time and time again in the Old Testament how God rejected and judged the Israelites because of sexual immorality and idol worship. God raised up their enemies to defeat and capture them. God gave them time to repent, and when they did, God had mercy on them

and restored them. The Bible declares, "Righteousness exalts a nation, but sin is a disgrace to any people" (Proverbs 14:34 NLT). We are to flee sexual immorality. Every other sin a person commits is outside the body, but the sexually immoral person sins against his or her own body. Glorify God in your body, which is a temple of the Holy Spirit.

- Unbelief in God and Jesus Christ is the world's sin
- The wages of sin is eternal death, but the gift of God is eternal life (Romans 6:3 NKJV).

The Antidote for Sin

- Put to death the sinful, earthly things lurking within you. Have nothing to do with sexual sin, impurity, lust, and shameful desires. Don't be greedy for the good things in life, for that is idolatry (Colossians 3:5 NLT).
- Believe that Jesus is the Son of God and came to set you free from sin.

- Accept Jesus into your heart as your Lord and Savior.
- Repent from you sins.
- Confess your sins to God.
- Accept God's grace for your salvation. You cannot earn it. It was paid for by the blood of Jesus Christ.
- Receive God's love and walk in freedom.
- Doing what the Bible says will set you free from sin.
- Put your trust in Jesus Christ.
- Focus on your reward in heaven as a child of God.

Chapter 9

Spiritual Warfare

You are in a spiritual battle whether you are aware or not. In my previous book, *Truth That Brings Peace, Love, Joy, and Hope*, I have a chapter devoted to spiritual warfare. I will expand on that in this book.

Your mind is a battlefield Satan is warring over to win. Victories in your life are won or lost in your mind. Satan constantly bombards us with negative thoughts. It is your responsibility to dispel wrong thoughts. You must think on purpose with a good attitude to excel in life. We become what we think about. Reading and studying the Word of God will help you think the way God wants you to think and act the way God wants you to act.

The scripture tells us in Ephesians 6:2

(NLT), "For we are not fighting against people made of flesh and blood, but against the evil rulers and authorities of the unseen world, against those mighty powers of darkness who rule this world, and against wicked spirits in the heavenly realms."

The Fall of Satan

Satan, also known as Lucifer or the devil, once held a high position in heaven as an archangel who led worship with the angels in heaven. Satan was created with musical instruments in his body. Satan's pride rose up, and he wanted to be like God. He desired to be worshipped. God instantly threw Satan from heaven unto the earth. Satan took one-third of the fallen angels with him; we call them demons. Satan has at his disposal millions of demons to do his work. Satan's job is to kill, steal, and destroy. He wants to kill your dreams as well as your God-given destiny. He also wants to steal your soul as well as your joy. He also wants to destroy your life. He will use all kinds of addictions such as alcohol, drugs, and strongholds to keep you in bondage. Satan knows your weaknesses! He has assigned demon spirits to study your family lineage to carry out his plan of destruction. I am not saying that all addictions are a result of demonic activity. Sometimes we bring on addictive problems and behaviors upon ourselves by what we consume.

These lineage spirits are called familiar spirits because they know your family history and weaknesses. They love to pass down curses from generation to generation.

If your family has had a history of health problems such as mental illness, heart problems, cancer, and others, chances are there may be some demonic activity associated with those diseases.

I can speak personally about mental illness. My mental illness started when I became addicted to opioids. I had suffered a disc tear from an automobile accident. My pain management doctor put me on opioid medicine. As the pain grew worse, he prescribed higher dosages. After several years, I became addicted to opioid medicine. I decided to live a more sedentary lifestyle. I would stay in bed a lot and sit on my recliner. I started to take less meds, and when I did, my body went into a full-blown bipolar disorder. I was in and out of six mental hospitals. I was unable to think reasonably or make decisions. I remember standing over the kitchen sink with a half-empty bottle of Ensure. I didn't want to drink the rest. I thought if I emptied it into the drain, it would clog it. I could not decide whether to throw it outside or not. I didn't want to wake my mother if I opened the door. I thought she would become very worried about me. I stood over the sink for almost two hours unable to make a decision. Finally, my mother woke up and told me to pour it down the sink.

Mental illness is a very cruel disease. First, you have a chemical imbalance, and you may never get the right medication that will help. Your mind is now an open door for demonic activity. Since you can't control your thoughts, the devil will send thoughts your way. He wants you to think that you will never get well and there is no hope for you. He will send thoughts that tell you your life is worthless and the best way out of your pain is suicide. He may also tell you to hurt others who have rejected you.

After going through six mental hospitals and

doctors, I lost hope. I thought that I would be institutionalized the rest of my life. For three years I was out of my mind. I would hear voices in my head that told me to kill myself. One day, while in a mental facility, I was looking at the sun. I saw it get bigger and bigger until it split into two suns. I knew that was not possible, but my eyes were seeing different. I was really in a bind; I couldn't trust what I was seeing or thinking. This was the absolute lowest point of my life.

After three years of being out of my mind, God's mercy stepped in. He sent me to the right psychiatrist who put me on the right medication. I slowly got better. I had a desire to read my Bible, listen to positive preaching from Joel Osteen, Joyce Meyer, and worship the Lord. God uses people and science to do his will. Sickness and disease do not come from God. More likely than not they are influenced by the devil.

I had also suffered with depression most of my life. God began a new work in me. He brought me out of the bipolar condition as well as delivered me from depression. I now feel better that I have ever felt.

God can use your pain to minister to others who are going through the same condition that you were delivered from. God is a healing God. He sent his Son to bear our sicknesses and diseases on the cross. "He took our sicknesses and removed our diseases" (Matthew 8:17 NLT).

God inspired me to write this book to help others.

God has designed a plan to defend and attack the demonic forces of evil. You are to put on all of God's armor so that you will be able to stand firm against all strategies and tricks of the devil (Ephesians 6:11 NLT). Use every piece of God's armor to resist the enemy in the time of evil so that after the battle you will be standing firm (Ephesians 6:13 NLT). Stand your ground, putting on the sturdy belt of truth and the body armor of God's righteousness. For shoes put on the peace that comes from the good news so that you will be fully prepared. In every battle you will need faith as your shield to stop the fiery arrows aimed at you by Satan. Put on salvation as your helmet, and take the sword of the Spirit, which is the Word of God (Ephesians 6:14–17 NLT).

You may notice that there is no armor to

protect your back side. You are to advance against the enemy and not retreat.

There are other ways to defeat the enemy. Humble yourselves before God. Resist the devil, and he will flee from you (James 4:7 NLT). If you have patience and peace, the devil can't do much to harm you. And the most important piece of clothing you must wear is love (Colossians 3:14 NLT). Love conquers all forces of evil. Fasting strengthens your spiritual man, making you more effective in the battle against the enemy. In Isaiah chapter 61 (NIV), the scriptures tell us to put on the garment of praise. God loves the praises of his people. Satan hates praise because he used to be the praise and worship leader in heaven.

I like to praise the Lord in the morning with praise and worship music. I get in my car to be alone and not bother anyone else. I crank up the music and sing to the Lord. After a while I feel God's peace come upon me. It makes my day more pleasant and productive.

During Jesus's ministry on earth, he used his authority to cast out demons and heal the sick and brokenhearted. When Jesus died on the cross and rose again, he gave Christians authority to do the same. "The truth is, anyone who believes in me will do the same works I have done, and even greater works, because I am going to be with the Father. You can ask for anything in my name, and I will do it" (John 14:12–13 NLT).

Chapter 10

God Is Love

Love defined in *The Merriam-Webster Dictionary* as: strong affection; unselfish loyal and benevolent concern for others.

God's love is unconditional, everlasting, pure, full of grace and mercy. No matter where you are and what you have done, God loves you. God formed you in your mother's womb. He cares about you and has a plan and purpose for your life. He knows everything about you because you are his creation. God has given you a unique fingerprint. No one else has your fingerprint, so it is with your life and how you are made. You are one of a kind.

God showed how he loved us by sending his only Son into the world so that we might have eternal life through him. This is real love. It is not that we loved God, but that he loved us and sent his Son as a sacrifice to take away our sins (1 John 4:9–10 NLT).

God is love, and all who live in love live in God, and God lives in them. And as we live in God, our love grows more perfect (1 John 4:16–17 NLT).

The more you grow in love, the less fear you feel because perfect love drives away fear. If we are afraid, it is for fear of judgment, and this shows that his love has not been perfected in us. We love one another because he loved us first (1 John 4:18–19 NLT).

What does love mean to a Christian? Love means doing what God has commanded us, and he has commanded us to love one another.

Everyone who believes that Jesus is the Christ is a child of God. And everyone who loves the Father loves his children too. We know we love God's children if we love God and obey his commands. Loving God means to keep his commandments, and that really isn't difficult (1 John 5:1–3 NLT).

God's love for us is so strong that he was willing to sacrifice his Son so we could enter his place of rest, heaven.

One can only imagine the pain that God went through to watch his Son go through the suffering and take upon himself the sins of the world as he was betrayed and crucified by his own people.

This is the kind of love God wants us to have. "Love is patient and kind. Love is not jealous or boastful or proud or rude. Love does not demand its own way. Love is not irritable, and it keeps no record of when it has been wronged. It is never glad about injustice but rejoices whenever the truth wins out. Love never gives up, never loses faith, is always hopeful, and endures through every circumstance" (1 Corinthians 13:4–7 NLT).

It is the love of God that draws sinners to self-repentance. God will never force his love upon you; he leaves it up to you to receive his love. God's love is always there for you. Ask God to receive his love. His love was poured out on Jesus Christ so that through Jesus your love can be made complete.

The greatest demonstration of God's love is that he loved everyone so much that he gave his only Son so that everyone who believes in him will not perish but have eternal life.

One of the amazing facts about God's love for us is that you can't earn it. Even though you may feel you don't deserve God's love, it is available to you. Just receive his mercy, his grace, and his love. God's love is with you always. You can depend on God to lead and guide you.

God's grace allows you to approach him boldly with your request.

When you confess your sins before God, he will remember them no more. His forgiveness is everlasting. All you have to do is ask.

God's grace is his unmerited favor and blessings because he loves you. Grace cannot be earned.

God's mercy is deserved punishment that is pardoned. God's grace and mercy are new every day. God does not give you grace and mercy ahead of time; it is only for today.

If you are not a Christian, you can do it now. Ask Jesus to forgive you of your sins. Invite him into your heart and follow him. You should get a Bible. I recommend the New Living Translation (NLT) because it is easy to read and understand. Begin reading in John, Psalms, Proverbs, and the New Testament. Read one chapter a day, or you just go at your own pace. Get into a good Bible-based church where you will be taught the Word of God.

Now that you have taken a stance to follow Jesus, beware your enemy the devil will come against you. Don't be surprised if family members and friends don't rejoice in your decision. You belong to God and Jesus Christ. You were bought with a high price. Becoming a Christian is the greatest decision you will ever make in life. Jesus will always be with you every step of the way. Call on him when you are in need and thank him for all that he has done and will do in your life.

Praise the Lord! Give thanks to the Lord, for he is good! His faithful love endures forever (Psalm 106:1 NLT).

As a Christian, you are highly favored by almighty God. His love, faithfulness, and blessings are for you to have. Receive it—it's your spiritual inheritance.

Sin is a hindrance to your spiritual inheritance. Repent for your sins and ask God to forgive you and then you can move into God's grace and abundance.

Chapter 11

Commandments of Jesus

Jesus said, "If you love me, obey my commandments" (John 14:15 NLT).

- The greatest commandment: Jesus said, "Love the Lord your God with all your heart and with all your soul, and with all your mind. A second is equally important: Love your neighbor as yourself" (Matthew 22:37–39 NLT).
- Treat others with respect, the way you want to be treated: Jesus said, "Do for others what you would like them to do for you. This is a summary of all that is taught in the law and the prophets" (Matthew 7:12 NLT).

- Forgive others: Jesus said, "Forgive anyone you are holding a grudge against, so that your Father in heaven will forgive your sins too" (Mark 11:25 NLT).

- You must be born again: "No one can enter the kingdom of God unless he is born of water and Spirit. Flesh gives birth to flesh, but the Spirit gives birth to Spirit. You should not be surprised at my saying, you must be born again" (John 3:5–7 NIV).

- "Remain in me and I will remain in you" (John 5:4 NLT). You cannot be fruitful apart from Jesus. "If you stay joined to me and my words remain in you, you may ask any request you like, and it will be granted!" (John 15:7 NLT).

- Let your light shine for all to see: "You are the light of the world—like a city on a mountain glowing in the night for all to see. Don't hide your light, let your good deeds shine out for all to see, so that everyone will praise your heavenly Father" (Matthew 5:14–16 NLT).

- Get rid of whatever causes you to sin: "If your right eye causes you to sin, gouge it out and throw it away. It is better for you to lose one part of your body than for your whole body to be thrown into hell. And if your right hand causes you to sin, cut it off and throw it away. It is better for you to lose part of your body than for you whole body to go into hell" (Matthew 5:29–30 NIV). The principle is not really to lose body parts but to get rid of things that cause you to sin. It may be immorality, lust, pride, envy, jealousy, unforgivingness, greed, or something else.

- Don't take revenge: Never pay back evil for evil to anyone. Do things in such a way that everyone can see you are honorable (Romans 12:15 NLT).
- Give to those who ask and don't turn away from those who want to borrow (Matthew 5:42 NLT).
- Love your enemies: Jesus said, "You have heard that the law of Moses says, 'Love your neighbor' and hate your enemy. But I say, love your enemies! Pray for those who persecute you! In that way, you will

be acting as true children of your Father in heaven" (Matthew 5:43–45 NLT).

- Give to please God, not to show off: don't do you good deeds publicly to be admired, because then you will lose the reward from your Father in heaven (Matthew 6:1 NLT).

- Pray in secret to your Father in heaven: Jesus said, "When you pray, go away by yourself, shut the door behind you and pray to your Father secretly. Then your Father who knows all secrets, will reward you" (Matthew 6:6 NLT).

- Remain in Jesus's love: "When you obey me, you remain in my love, just as I obey my Father and remain in his love" (John 15:10 NLT).

- Jesus's example of how you should pray: "Our Father in heaven, may your name be honored. May your kingdom come soon. May your will be done here on earth, just as it is in heaven. Give us our food for today, and forgive us our sins, just as we have forgiven those who have sinned against us and don't let us yield to temptation, but deliver us from the evil one" (Matthew 6:9–13 NLT).

- Fast: Jesus said, "When you fast, don't make it obvious as the hypocrites do, who try to look pale and disheveled. But when you fast, comb your hair and wash your face. Then no one will suspect you are fasting except your Father, who knows what you do in secret. And your Father who knows all secrets will reward you" (Matthew 6:16–18 NLT). Fasting is a way to humble yourself before God. It strengthens your spiritual man and brings your worldly nature under control. Fasting is spiritual warfare against your enemy, Satan. Beside food there are other areas you can fast, such as television, electronics, and social media.

- Money and possessions: "Don't store up treasures here on earth, where they can be eaten by moths and get rusty, and where thieves break in and steal. Store your treasures in heaven, where they will never become moth-eaten or rusty and they will be safe from thieves. Wherever your treasure is, there your heart and thoughts will also be" (Matthew 6:19–21 NLT). You can store up treasure in heaven when you give to the poor, orphans, widows, those who need food, water, or other needs. There are many ministries that do just that. When you give your resources (time and money) to such ministries, you are storing up treasures in heaven for yourself.

- Don't worry about your needs: Jesus said, "So I tell you don't worry about everyday life—whether you have enough food, drink, and clothes. Doesn't life consist of more than food and clothing? Can all your worries add a single moment to your life? Of course not. Your heavenly Father already knows all your needs, and he will give you all you need from day to day if you live for him and make the Kingdom your primary concern. So don't worry about tomorrow, for tomorrow will bring its own worries. Today's trouble is enough for today" (Matthew 6:25–34 NLT). God gives you grace for today.

- Do not judge others: "Stop judging others, and you will not be judged. For others will treat you as you treat them. Whatever measure you use to judge others, it will be used to measure how you are judged (Matthew 7:1-2 NLT).

- Pray effectively: "Keep on asking, and you will be given what you ask for. Keep on looking, and you will find. Keep on knocking, and the door will be opened. For everyone who asks receives. Everyone who seeks, finds. And the door is opened to everyone who knocks (Matthew 7:7-8 NLT). Jesus wants you to be persistent in prayer with faith and thanksgiving.

- Care for the needy: You are to feed the hungry, give water to the thirsty, welcome strangers into your home, give clothing to those who need, care for the sick, and visit those in prison. You may ask, "How can I do all those things?" You can do this by giving to ministries that are involved in meeting the needs of people and you can also volunteer.

- Enter the narrow gate to God's kingdom: "You can enter God's Kingdom only through the narrow gate. The highway to hell is broad, and its gate is wide for the many who choose the easy way. But the gateway to life is small, and the road is narrow, and only a few ever find it" (Matthew 7:13–14 NLT).

- Use your spiritual authority: Jesus called his twelve disciples to him and gave them authority to cast out evil spirits and to heal every kind of disease and illness. "Go and announce to them that the Kingdom of Heaven is near. Heal the sick, raise the dead, cure those with leprosy, and cast out demons. Give as freely as you have received!" (Matthew 10:7–8 NLT). The same authority Jesus gave to his disciples is available to Christians. You must go out in faith and believe as the disciples did and do the will of God.

- Do not exalt yourself: If you want to be great in the kingdom of God, you must be a servant to others. Jesus said, "The greatest among you must be a servant. But those who exalt themselves will be humbled, and those who humble themselves will be exalted" (Matthew 23:11–12 NLT).

- Settle conflicts with others: "Confess your sins to each other and pray for each other so that you may be healed" (James 5:16 NLT). A lot of times the conflict is trivial. It could be a communication error, too prideful to receive correction, or hurt feelings.

- Have faith in God: Jesus said to his disciples, "Have faith in God. I assure you that you can say to this mountain, 'May God lift you up and throw you into the sea,' and your command will be obeyed. All that is required is that you really believe and do not doubt in your heart. Listen to me! You can pray for anything, and if you believe, you will have it" (Mark 11:22–24 NLT).

- Love one another: "I command you to love each other in the same way that I love you. And here is how to measure it— the greatest love is shown when people lay down their lives for their friends. You are my friends if you obey me" (John 15:12–14 NLT).

- Remember the covenant of Jesus: Jesus took a loaf of bread; and when he had thanked God for it, he broke it in pieces and gave it to the disciples, saying, "This is my body, given to you. Do this in remembrance of me" (Luke 22:19 NLT). After supper he took another cup of wine and said, "This wine is the token of God's new covenant to save you—an agreement sealed with the blood I will pour out for you" (Luke 22:20 NLT).

- Show mercy: "Be merciful, just as your Father is merciful" (Luke 6:36 NIV). Mercy means compassion shown to an offender. God gives mercy to sinners who repent. They should have gotten punishment, but God pardons them of their sins. You must do accordingly to others who sin against you. You must show mercy to those in need and help them.

- Go and make disciples: Jesus said, "I have been given complete authority in heaven and on earth. Therefore go and make disciples of all nations, baptizing them in the name of the Father and the Son and the Holy Spirit. Teach these new disciples to obey all the commands I have given you. And be sure of this: I am with you always, even to the end of the ages" (Matthew 28:18–20 NLT).

- You must be ready: "You must be ready all the time, for the Son of Man will come when least expected" (Luke 12:40 NLT). Jesus is coming back a second time to rule and reign over the earth. Will you be ready—doing the will of God—when he returns?

- Repent: "Turn from your sins and turn to God, because the Kingdom of Heaven is near" (Matthew 4:17 NLT).

- Pray for more workers in God's harvest field: "The harvest is so great, but the workers are so few. So pray to the Lord who is in charge of the harvest; ask him to send more workers for his fields" (Matthew 9:37–38 NLT).

- Don't be greedy: "Watch out! Be on your guard against all kinds of greed; a man's life does not consist in the abundance of his possessions" (Luke 12:15 NIV).

- Do no lust: "Anyone who even looks at a woman with lust in his eyes has already committed adultery with her in his heart"

(Matthew 5:28 NLT). This applies to women as well.

- You must have faith: "Without faith it is impossible to please Him, for he who comes to God must believe that He is, and that He is a rewarder of those who diligently seek Him" (Hebrews 11:6 NKJV). By faith you must believe before you receive what you asked for.

- Deny yourself and follow Jesus: "If any of you wants to be my follower, you must put aside your selfish ambitions, shoulder you cross daily, and follow me. If you try to keep your life for yourself, you will lose it. But if you give up your life for me, you will find true life. And how do you benefit if you gain the whole world but lose or forfeit your own soul in the process?" (Luke 9:23–25 NLT).

Chapter 12

Personal Affirmations of Who You Are in Christ

You will need to know who you are in Christ to break through insecurity and pride to reach your God given destiny. The Word of God says, "God resist the proud. But gives grace to the humble" (James 4:6 NKJV). You can only reach your full destiny when you conquer pride and insecurity.

You must repent of your sins or this will be a stumbling block for your future.

When you break these strongholds, God will promote you to a new level.

Personal affirmations that will help you in your walk with Jesus Christ:

- The Lord himself watches over me.
- I can do all things through Christ (Philippians 4:13 NKJV).
- Jesus gives me the strength I need to accomplish my goals.
- The favor of God is upon me; I am highly favored.
- God's grace and mercy are with me every day.
- The peace of Jesus Christ lives within me.
- I am a child of God (Romans 8:10 NKJV).
- I am right with God through faith in Jesus Christ (Romans 3:22 NKJV).
- I am a member of the body of Christ.
- I am God's masterpiece (Ephesians 2:10 NLT).
- I am a citizen of heaven (Philippians 3:20 NLT).
- I have access to God through the Holy Spirit (Ephesians 2:18 NLT).
- I am free from the bondage of sin (Romans 6:22 NLT).
- I am free from condemnation (Romans 8:1 NLT).
- Good deeds will come from my life.

- God's love is always with me.
- I have God's power and love working in me.
- I have a sound mind and self-control.
- I am a witness of Christ.
- My body is a temple of the Holy Spirit (1 Corinthians 6:19 NIV).
- The Lord will take care of all my needs.
- I trust God.
- I can come bodily with my request before God's throne of grace.
- The joy of the Lord is my strength (Nehemiah 8:10 NLT).
- With God all things are possible.
- I have angels protecting me.
- I have authority to use Jesus's name.
- I am made righteous through the blood of Jesus (Romans 3:25 NLT).
- God has a purpose and plan for my life— plans to prosper me and keep me from harm (Jeremiah 29:11 NIV).
- God's love for me is unconditional.
- God is with me, God is helping me, and God is guiding me.
- God's blessings will chase me down.

- I am equipped and well able to do what God called me to do.
- No weapon formed against me by the devil will prosper (Isaiah 53:17 NKJV).

Conclusion

The greatest gift you can give God and Jesus is yourself. By giving your life to God and receiving Jesus as your Lord and Savior, you become a child of God. God loves his children and is always looking for ways to bless them. God and Jesus are really excited that you will spend eternity with them in heaven. Remember that Jesus paid for your admission to heaven by dying on the cross for your sins. You belong to God and Jesus Christ. Your heavenly prize awaits you for the good deeds you have done after salvation.

If you have not invited Jesus into your heart to be your Lord and Savior, you can do it now. Simply say, "Lord Jesus, I invite you to be a part of my life; come into my heart. I ask you to forgive me of my sins. I turn to you and away from my sinful life. I will now follow you all the days of my life. Amen."

Your walk with Jesus has begun. He has given you a measure of faith and will help you through every circumstance in life if you ask him. He will help you develop your faith into maturity as trials and circumstances come your way so that you can fulfill your God-given destiny.

The devil will come against you when you become a Christian. Stand firm and rely on your faith that Jesus will help you. The Spirit of God who lives in you is greater than the devil.

When you are saved, the Holy Spirit lives in you. He will lead and guide you into all truth. He is there to advise you to do something or to avoid danger. To hear from the Holy Spirit, you must spend time reading and knowing the Word of God, have a thankful heart, and worship God and Jesus Christ. Go to a quiet place and ask the Holy Spirit to speak to you. Take a journal with you and write down what the Spirit is saying to you. It will take time and patience, but soon you will learn to hear his voice. It is not an audible voice but an impression in your heart. You will find your life will run a lot more smoothly and peacefully.

Remember to flee from temptation and turn to God for his grace and mercy. Temptations that come into your life are no different from what others experience. And God is faithful. He will keep the temptation from becoming so strong that you can't stand up against it. When you are tempted, he will show you a way out so that you will not give in to it (1 Corinthians 10:13 NLT). The more you give into the temptation and sin, the more it becomes a stronghold in your life. Jesus came so that you can be set free from the bondage of sin.

Always give thanks to God, Jesus, and the Holy Spirit for what they have done and will do in your life. Pray for God's wisdom, favor, anointing, and blessings. You will be amazed at the results. May God's peace, love, joy, and hope be with you.

I want to thank my intercessors who helped pray this book through. I met a lot of opposition from Satan, but with the prayers and support of my prayer partners, we were able to overcome obstacles in our path. A special thanks to Pastor

Farley Painter, Crestward Broussard, and Priscilla Cormier.

My hope is that this book has blessed you and helped you decide to receive Jesus Christ as your Lord and Savior. You can help your family and friends by purchasing this book to help them discover who Jesus really is. God bless you, and may the peace of Jesus Christ, the Prince of Peace, reside in your heart and guide you in your life. This book is available wherever books are sold.

About the Author

Jerry Gaspard grew up in a small rural community in South Louisiana, known as Cajun Country. He was raised on a rice and cattle farm and the family owned a grocery store in Forked Island, Louisiana. Jerry played sports in high school - basketball, baseball, and track. He graduated from Louisiana State University with a B.S. in Vocational Agriculture Education and the school of hard knocks. Jerry's hobbies include watching LSU baseball, football, and softball, the New England Patriots, the New Orleans Saints, and the New York Yankees. He also enjoys gardening and playing with his cat, Princess. Jerry is also a student of the Bible and loves to read inspirational books and watch inspirational movies.

Jerry has also authored another book, "Truth That Brings Peace, Love, Joy And Hope", it is available where books are sold.

Printed in the United States
by Baker & Taylor Publisher Services